RUBANK EDUCATIONAL LIBRARY No. 144

# Concert and Contest COLLECTION

for

## Bb CLARINET

with piano accompaniment

Compiled and Edited

by **H. VOXMAN**

**RUBANK** ®

**HAL•LEONARD**® CORPORATION

7777 W BLUEMOUND RD PO BOX 13819 MILWAUKEE, WI 53213

# Contents

**CONCERT AND CONTEST COLLECTION for Clarinet**

# Allegretto Fantasia

**B♭ Clarinet**

SEXTUS MISKOW
Edited by H. Voxman

Copyright MCMXLVIII by Rubank, Inc., Chicago, Ill.
International Copyright Secured

# Adagio

from
## Concerto for Clarinet, K.622

**Bb Clarinet**

W. A. MOZART
Edited by H. Voxman

Adagio (♩=42)

# B♭ Clarinet

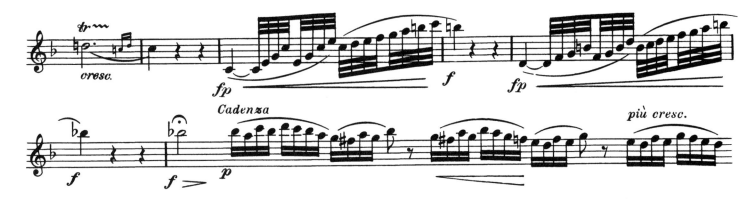

6

# Allegretto Grazioso

from

## Sonata in F Minor

**B♭ Clarinet**

J. BRAHMS, Op. 120. No. 1
Edited by H. Voxman

Allegretto grazioso

*grazioso e dolcissimo sempre*

## Bb Clarinet

# Nocturne

from
Concerto in G Minor

Bb Clarinet

TH. VERHEY, Op. 47
Edited by H. Voxman

# Bb Clarinet

**Tempo I**

# Fantasy-Piece

**Bb Clarinet**

R. SCHUMANN, Op. 73, No. 1
Edited by H. Voxman

## B♭ Clarinet

# Aria and Scherzo

Bb Clarinet

AGOSTINO GABUCCI
Edited by H. Voxman

# Bb Clarinet

# 14
# Promenade

**Bb Clarinet**

MARC DELMAS
Edited by H. Voxman

# Chanson

**Bb Clarinet**

R. GLIERE, Op. 35, No. 3
Edited by H. Voxman

# Nocturne

B♭ Clarinet

L. BASSI
Revised by H. Voxman

**B♭ Clarinet**

*meno mosso*

Tempo I

*poco più mosso*

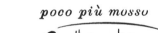

*a tempo*

# Menuet
## from
### Divertimento in D, K.334

**Bb Clarinet**

W. A. MOZART
Edited by H. Voxman

**B♭ Clarinet**

# Canzonetta

**Bᵇ Clarinet**

GABRIEL PIERNÉ, Op. 19
Edited by H. Voxman

Andantino moderato (♩. = 60)
*Avec élégance*

un poco rubato

8

poco rit. a tempo

1

1

Bb Clarinet

# Scherzo in C Minor

Bb Clarinet

PAUL KOEPKE
Edited by H. Voxman

Allegro

Meno mosso

# Bb Clarinet

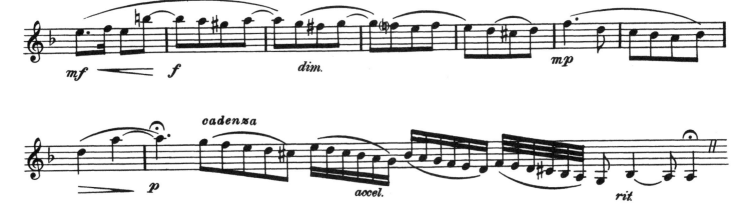

# <sup>24</sup> Ballade

**B♭ Clarinet**

NIELS W. GADE, Op. 43, No. 3
Edited by H. Voxman

# Scene and Air
## from
## Luisa di Montfort

**Bb Clarinet**

MICHAEL BERGSON, Op.82
Edited by H. Voxman

To reduce performance time cut from (A) to (B) using modulation indicated.

## B♭ Clarinet

CODA

*variante*

*Fine*

# Romance

Bb Clarinet

JEAN BECKER, Op. 3
Edited by H. Voxman